Sense
Of the Isle

Verse
by
Louis Chelton

Map and Drawings
by
Wilson Ware

Photographs
by
Susan Zorn Chelton
Dudley Chelton
Cole Chelton
and
Louis Chelton

ISBN: 978-0-9789271-8-9

Elden Publishing, LLC

In Memory of Wilson Ware,
My island mentor.

Table of Contents

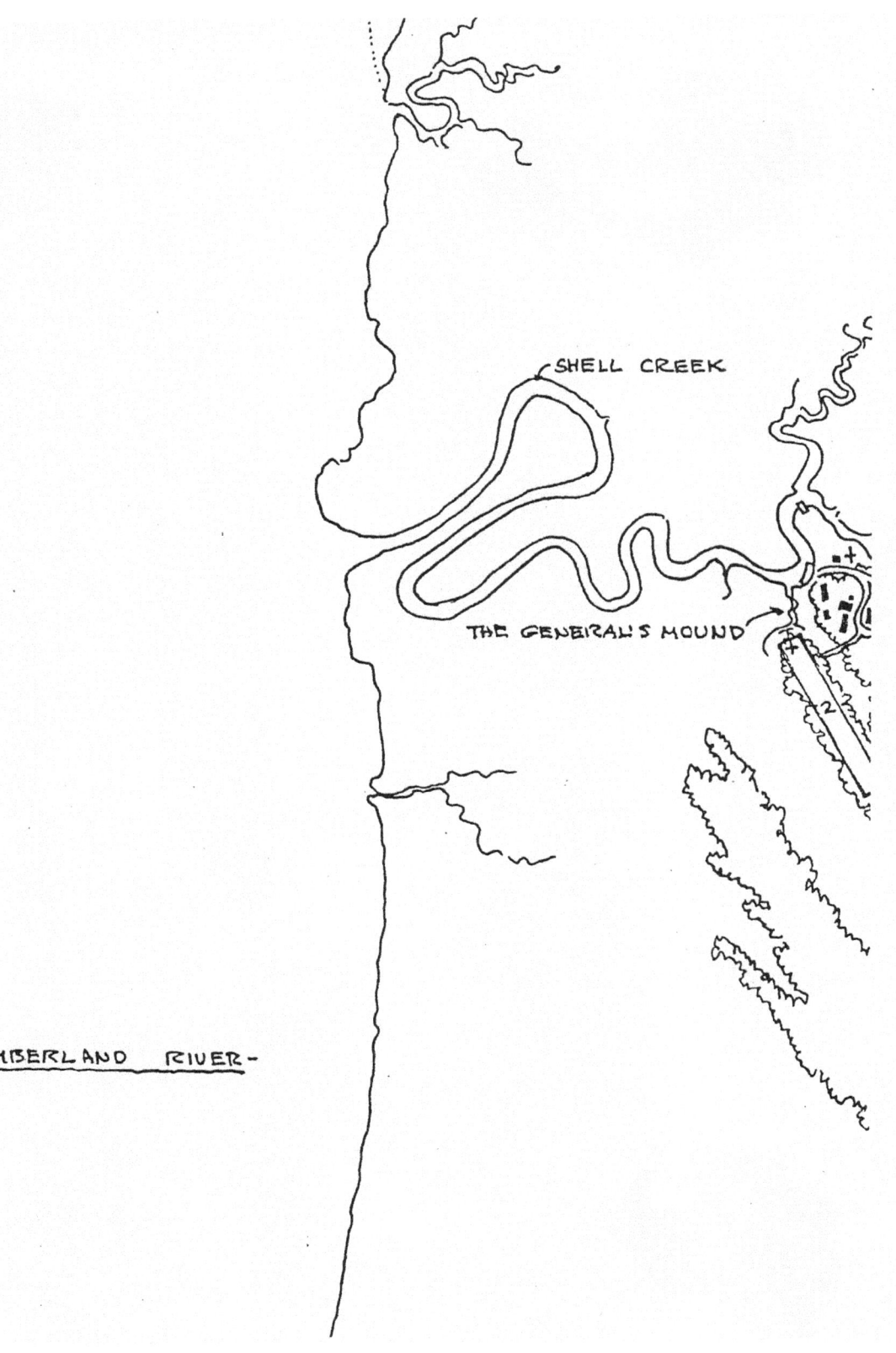

SHELL CREEK

THE GENERAL'S MOUND

- CUMBERLAND RIVER -

6

Shell Creek

The rough chop
That slides the ice chest
Across the deck
Subsides...
At the mouth of the creek,
The engine's din
Drops to drone.
The wind which swept spray
Onto my tinted lenses
Falls away
Like the shades from my face,
Warm greens and brown
Wash over bare eyes
In the gentler light
Of this cradle of reeds.

The way winds
From where we are
To where we have been
And back.
"Straight" is an abstract
On this short journey
That is longer and deeper
Than any so far.
Murmured speech
And the sounds of sea fowl
Decorate the boat's even song.
With each breath
The shirt
Grows light
On my shoulders.

The dock grows large,
The engine idles, rumbles, idles,
Lines and banter fly
Cargo streams from hold
To hand to hand
Amid jokes, new and old,
A giddy moment of arrival
Fades into calm and the clicking of fiddlers
As the dank shell fragrance
Wafts "there"
Gently into here.

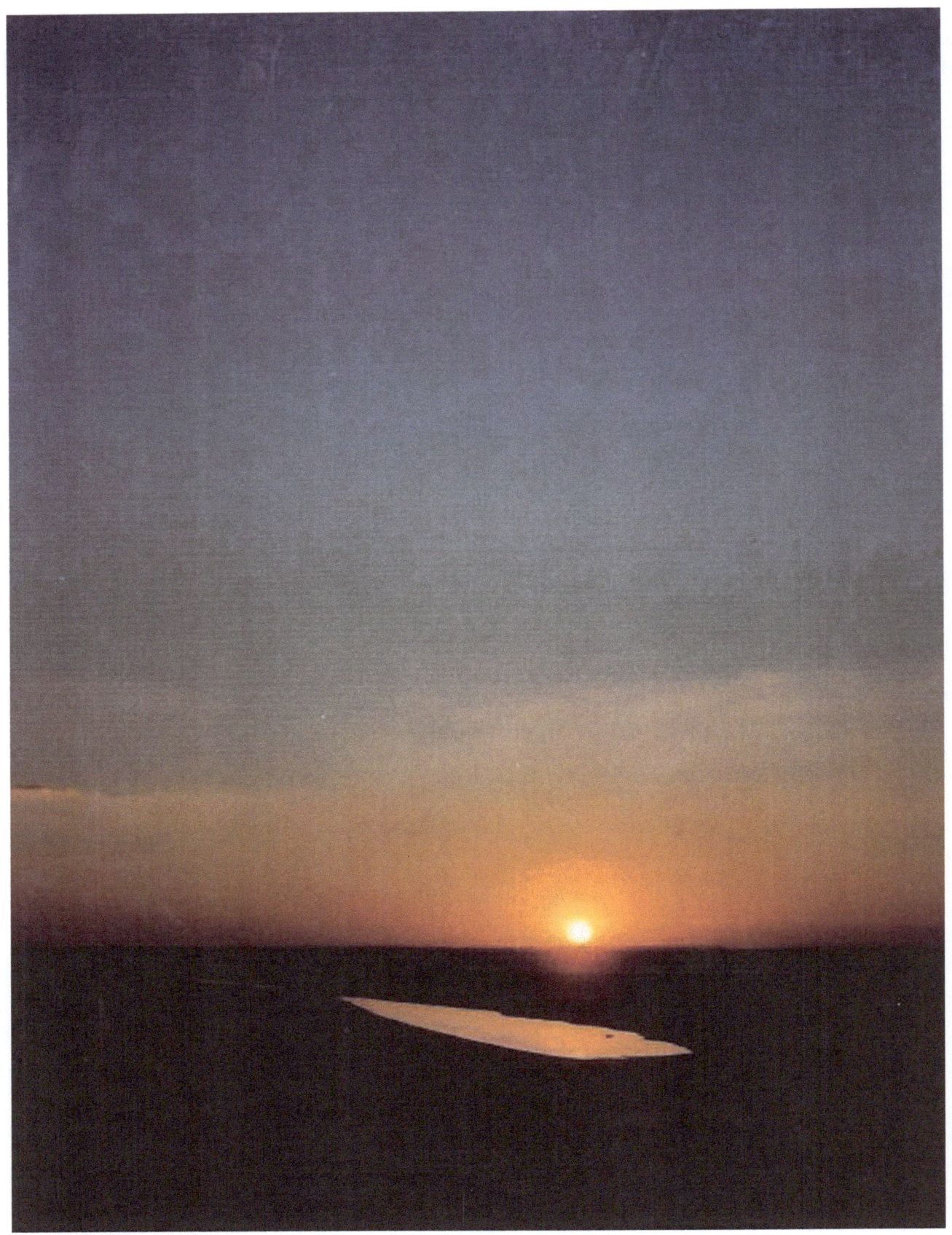

One Sense

My ears reach behind me
To the motions of the marsh
My eyes reach forward
To the stars
I feel, breathe, taste
The cool alchemic cadence
Of the universe
I am close and far
Close
And far

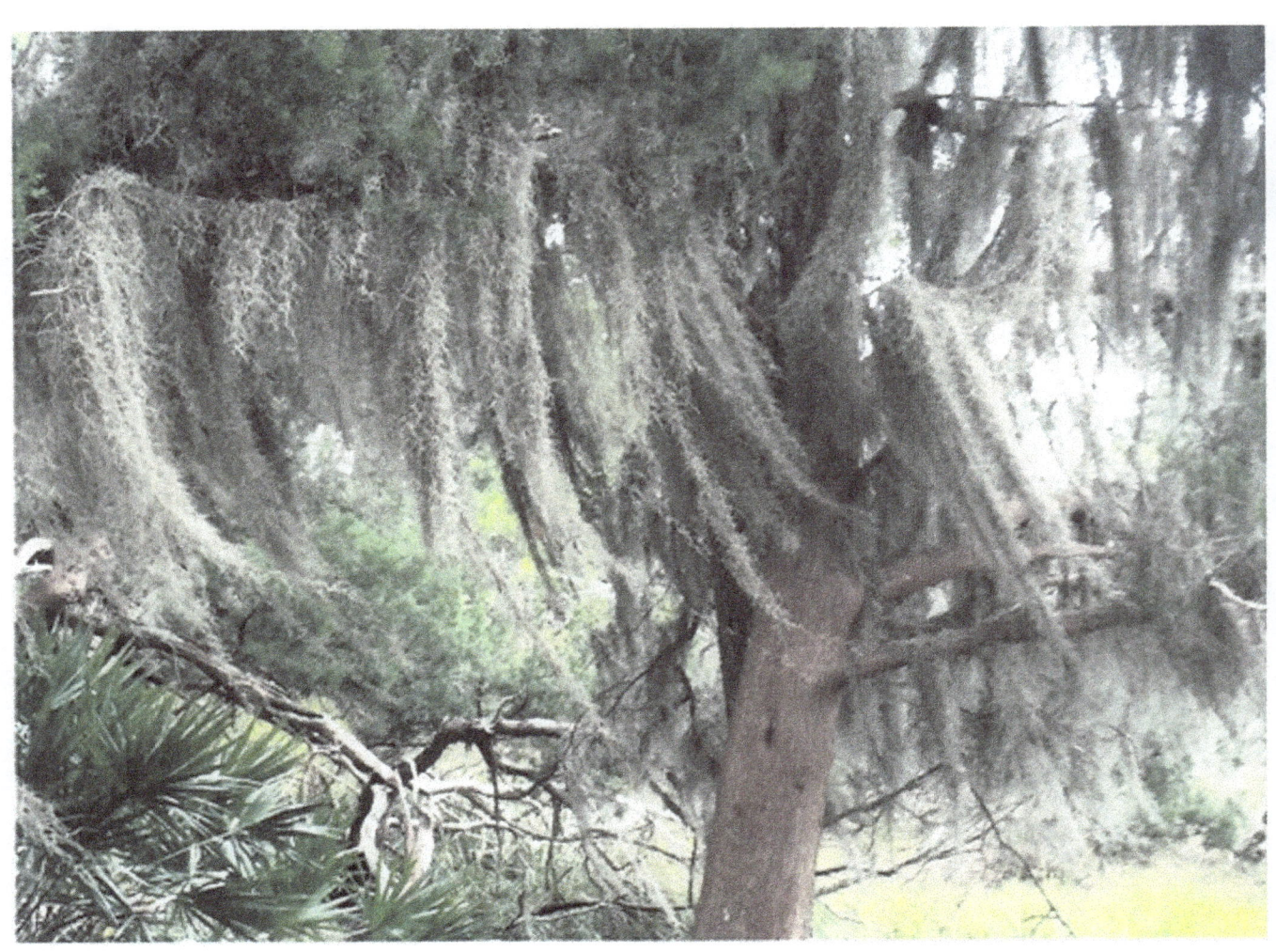

Air Borne

The wind lifts and carries
My mind
My skin
My hair
Buffeted, pressed
I fly standing
Through air
Smell sweet
Bird fleet
Wings at my side

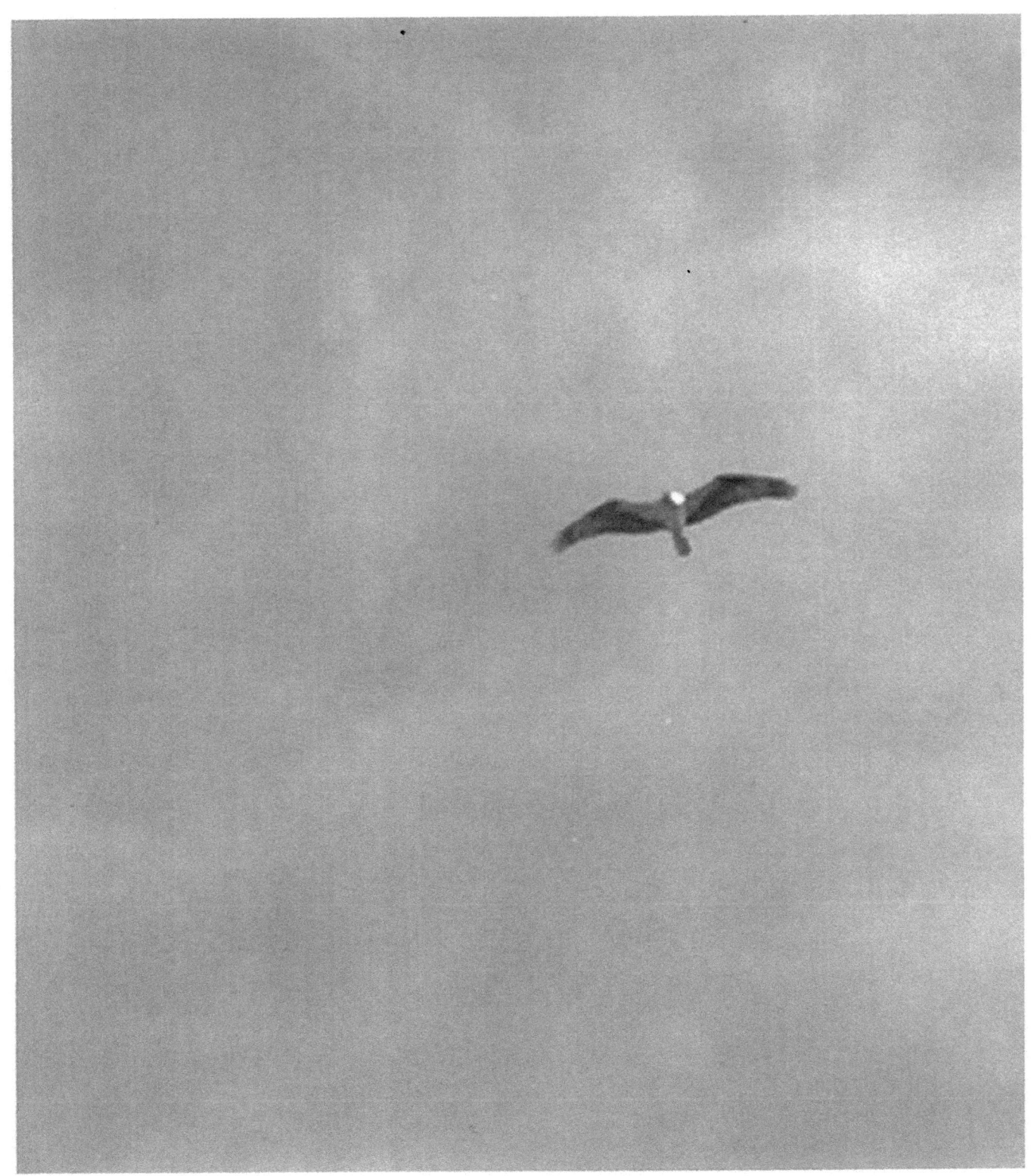

Osprey

"Beautiful creature!"
Hung still in the wind
That cools my back,
I speak to you
With my one encaverned wing,
My full head
Craves the freedom
Of your hollow bones

I whisper my call,
"I love you"
And your dip and hover,
Your shaken feathers,
For one brief moment,
For one small height
Take me with you

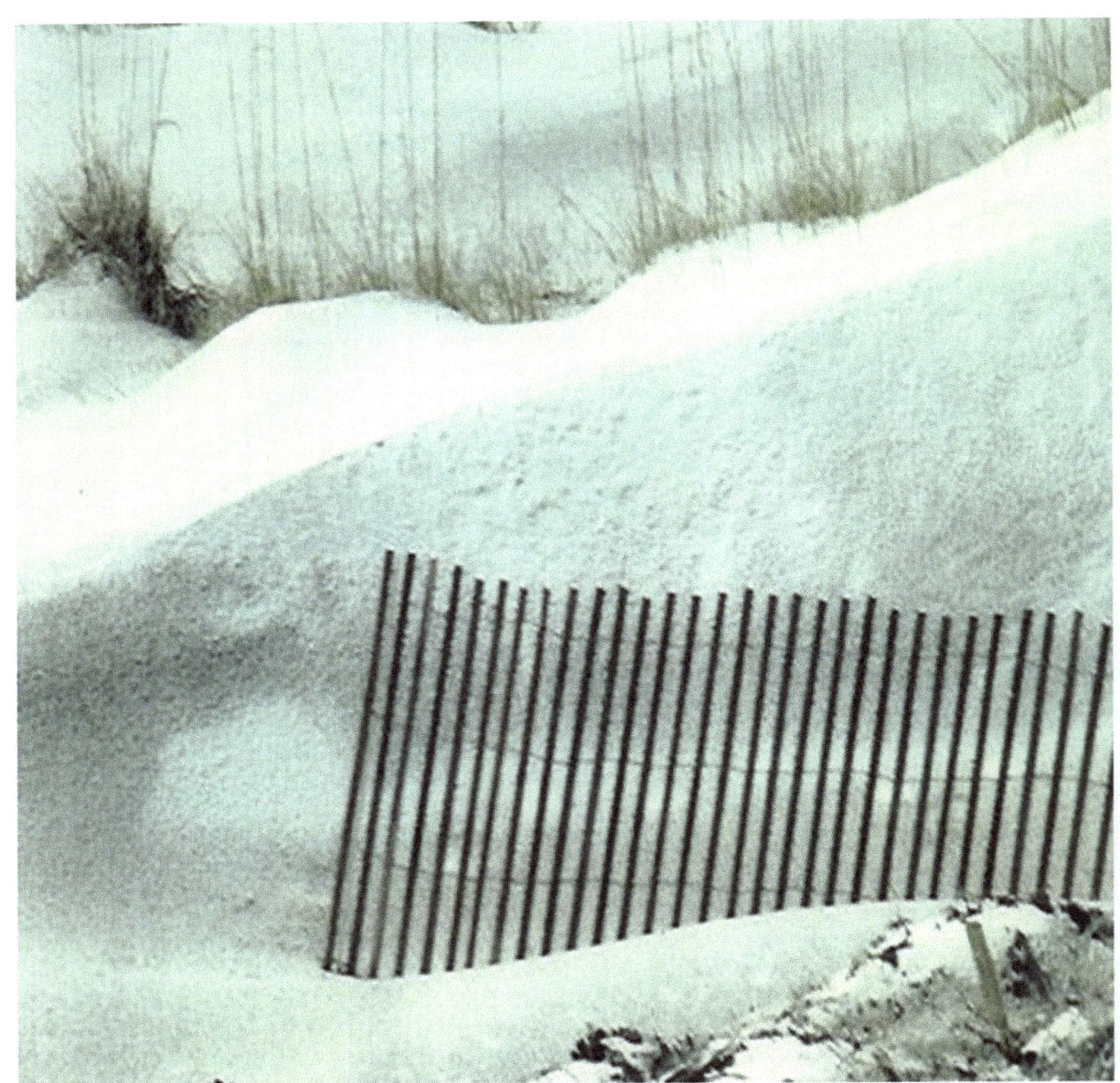

rosio

The wind whips sand fronds
From the crest of the dune
Cascading grains collapse
And pack
                And stack
And feign to climb once more
                    To the peak
But to tumble back under
The crumbling brow

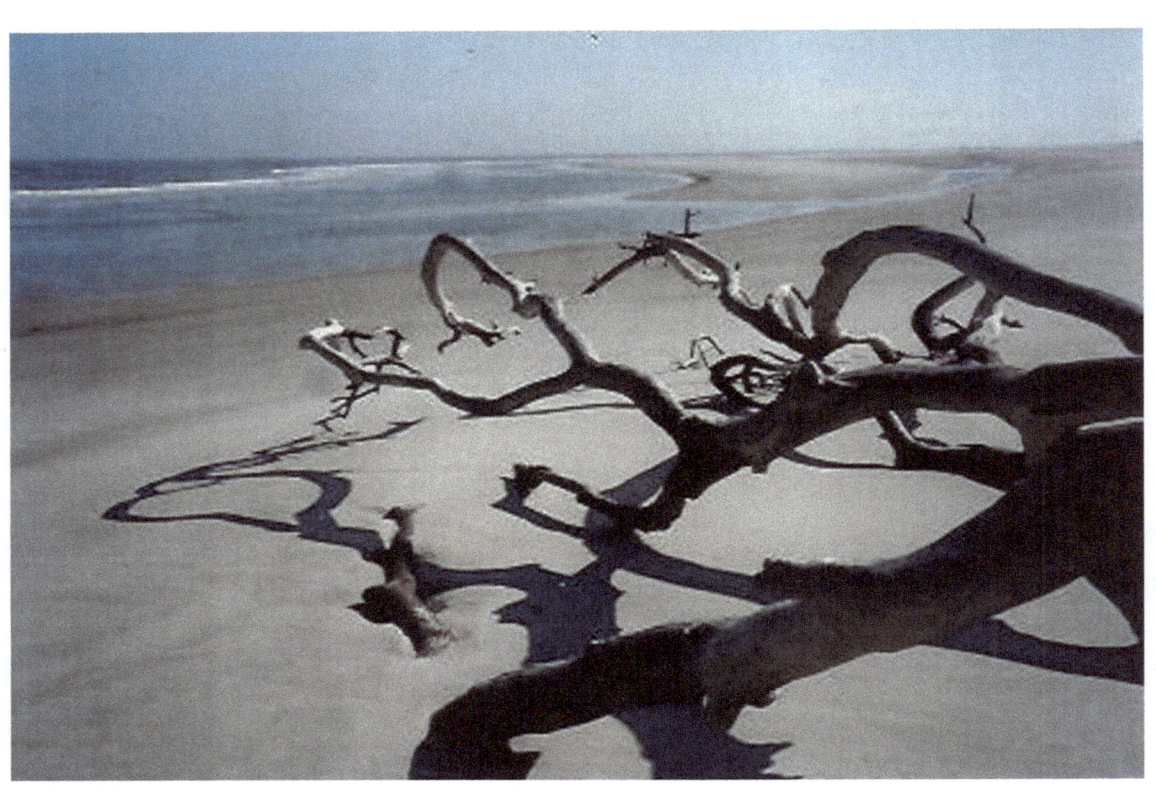

Driftwood

On the north beach the dunes
Fall into the sea
The sun sands a pale finish
On roots and limbs
A strewn tangle
Of white and gray
That short yards away
And above
Strands green

I wander among these frameworks of lives
Nearing trance

Swirling grain forms faces, fauna
Diverging roots reunite
And merge
Stark shadows
Cast on glowing sand
Spin shapes in the mind
Of the ancient
And the eternal
And the everyday

From behind and below
The waters lap in hunger
The peaceful murmur
Of relentless digestion
That brings this all back to sand,
And the waters
Shift the sands
Where they will

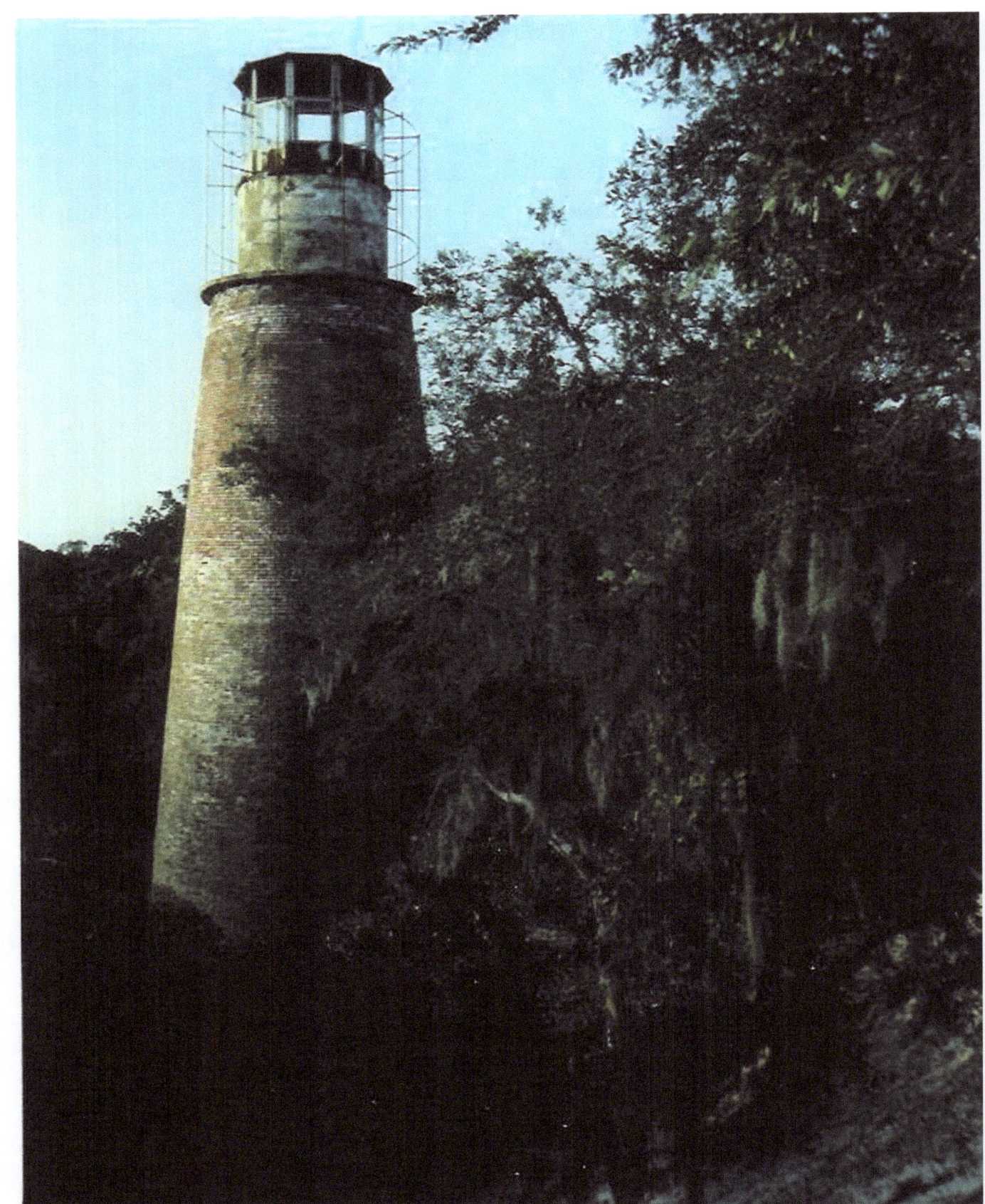

Here Not "There"

The magic is here tonight.
I planned to court the driftwood's spell
But the wind drew me on
Past the roughened swell
With a fluid line of pelican flight
To the point
Where the lighthouse once threw light

Burnished band of churning waters
Bronzed by setting sun
Tempts my gaze
As if to fall within a photo's frame . . .
But the wind brings a cry!
Drawing my eye to the wing
Of a skimmer—no three!
Who joust and vie
In crisp arcs of flight
Flashes of black then white

Self sense flickers, fades out
Gone like the great lantern's beam
Dark and silent
Brick tower, man
Stand in wind
With dunes and trees
Part, not force
In the moment eternal

You knew, we know
That the greatest things
We have
on this island
Are those
We cannot possess

Goodbye Wilson
You are alive in our thoughts.

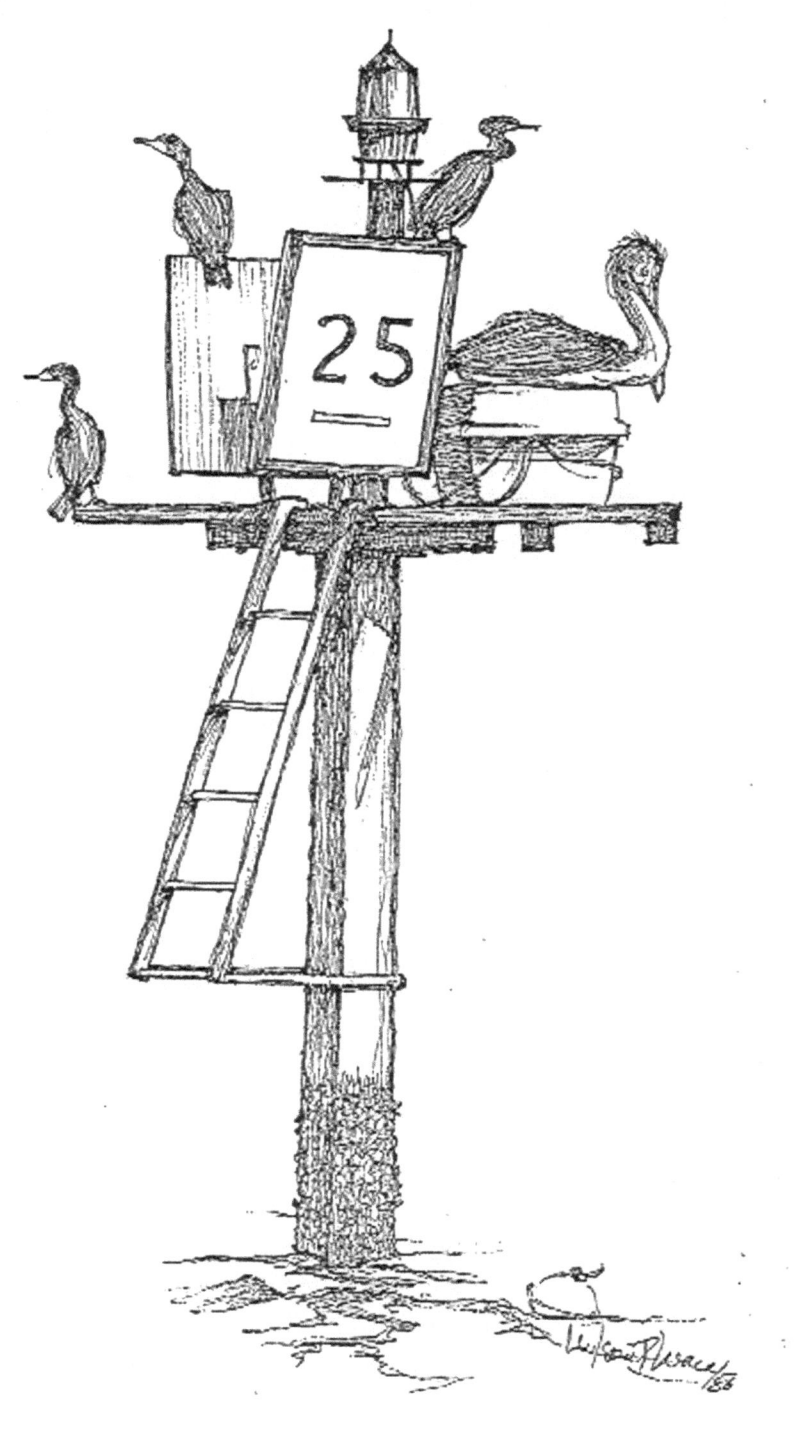

Island Observations

Island Observations

Island Observations

Island Observations

Island Observations

Island Observations

Island Observations

Island Observations

www.ingramcontent.com/pod-product-compliance
Lightning Source LLC
Chambersburg PA
CBHW052137170526
45162CB00004B/41